W9-BWV-830

ALBANIA

MAJOR WORLD NATIONS

ALBANIA

Aaron E. Lear

CHELSEA HOUSE PUBLISHERS
Philadelphia

J 96
914
Leon

Chelsea House Publishers
http://www.chelseahouse.com

Copyright © 2000, 2001 by Chelsea House Publishers,
a subsidiary of Haights Cross Communications.
All rights reserved.
Printed in Malaysia

3 5 7 9 8 6 4

Library of Congress Cataloging-in-Publication Data

Lear, Aaron.
Albania / Aaron E. Lear.
p.   cm. — (Major world nations)
Includes index.
Summary: Examines the history, geography, and cultural developments of this
European nation bordering the Adriatic Sea and the former Yugoslavia.

ISBN 0-7910-4754-7
1. Albania—Juvenile literature. [1. Albania.] I. Title.
II. Series.
DR910.L43   1999
949.65—dc21   99-15680
CIP

ACKNOWLEDGEMENTS

The Author and Publishers are grateful to the following sources for information and
photographs: Albanian Orthodox Archdiocese, Boston; AP/Wide World Photo;
Library of Congress; National Archives; UPI Newsphoto; Malcolm Gilson/Black Star;
H. Armstrong Roberts. Picture Research: Imagefinders, Inc.; PAR/NYC.

30652001149410

CONTENTS

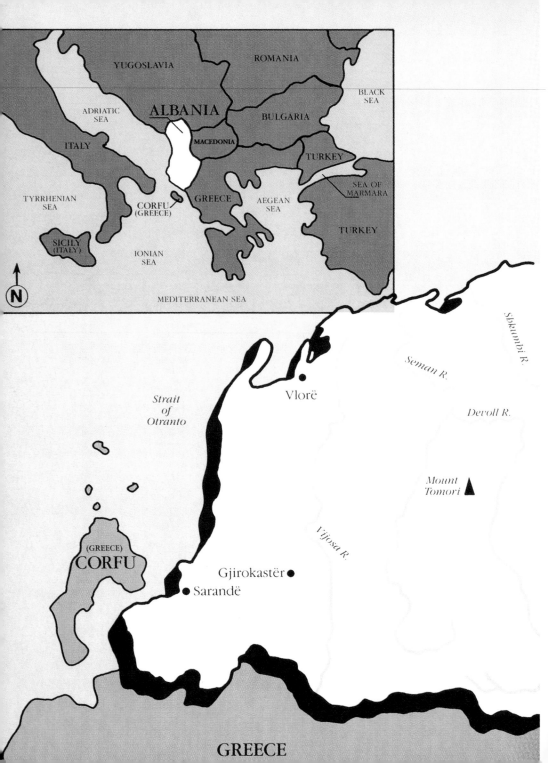

FACTS AT A GLANCE

Land and People

Official Name	Republic of Albania
Location	Southeastern Europe on the Balkan Peninsula
Area	11,000 square miles (27,748 square kilometers)
Climate	Temperate
Capital	Tirana
Other Cities	Durrës, Elbasan
Population	3,293,000
Population Distribution	Urban, 42.4 percent; rural, 57.6 percent
Major Rivers	Vijosa, Mati, Drin, Drin i zi, Buene, Seman, Devoll, Shkumbi
Major Lakes	Shkodër, Ohrid, Prespa
Mountains	Northern Albanian, Tomori, Acroceraunian, Chimara
Highest Point	Mount Korab, 9,068 feet (2,764 meters)
Official Language	Albanian

Ethnic Groups	Albanians, 98 percent; Greeks, 1.8 percent
Religions	Muslim (65 percent), Orthodox Christian, Roman Catholic
Literacy Rate	91.8 percent
Average Life Expectancy	Male, 68.5 years; female, 74.3 years

Economy

Natural Resources	Hydroelectric power, chromium, copper, brown coal, crude petroleum, natural gas
Agricultural Products	Wheat, corn, oats, legumes, sugar beets, cotton, tobacco, potatoes, fruits, sunflower seeds
Industries	Refining of chrome, copper, petroleum; petrochemicals
Major Imports	Food, manufactured goods, mineral fuels
Major Exports	Chrome ore, copper products, fruits and vegetables, crude materials
Major Trading Partners	Italy, Greece, Turkey
Currency	Lek

Government

Form of Government	Unitary Republic
Government Bodies	People's Assembly
Formal Head of State	President
Head of Government	Prime Minister

HISTORY AT A GLANCE

late 3rd century B.C.	The Illyrians, an ancient Indo-European people, form a powerful kingdom of small tribes on the Balkan Peninsula under Argon.
167 B.C.	The Romans conquer all of Illyria.
167 B.C.-395 A.D.	Illyria becomes an important part of the Roman Empire.
395 A.D.	Illyria becomes part of the Byzantine Empire after the fall of the Roman Empire.
3rd-5th centuries	The Huns and Visigoths overrun most of the Balkan Peninsula. The Slavic culture eventually absorbs all the Illyrian tribes except in the region of present-day Albania.
14th century	Serbian king Stephen Dushan incorporates Albania into his empire.
1430	The Turkish Empire gains control over all of Albania. Its feudal lords become vassals of the Turkish sultan. The sons of the lords are taken by the Turks and raised in the Turkish religion and traditions.

1443	One of the lords' sons, Scanderbeg, who excelled in his training by the Turks, returns to Albania, renounces the Muslim religion, and declares a holy war against the Turks.
1443-1468	The Albanians unite behind Scanderbeg and with the support of the Roman Catholic Church manage to liberate most of the country.
1468	Scanderbeg dies and the Turkish sultans gradually retake the country.
18th century	Over centuries of Turkish rule, Albania has gradually become divided into many individual estates each ruled by an Albanian Muslim landlord. The landlords or *beys* often fight among themselves keeping the country divided and easily controlled by the Turks.
mid-19th century	An independence movement begins and nationalist groups emerge among Albanians living in other countries.
1908	The Albanians finally revolt against the Turks and four years of intermittent fighting follows.
1912	On November 12 Albania proclaims its independence. Ismail Kemal Bey Vlora heads a provisional government.
1913	The European Conference of Ambassadors decides that because of the inexperience of its leaders Albania should have a monarch. A German prince, William of Wied, is selected king.
1914	Essad Pasha, a powerful feudal leader, leads a rebellion against the new king and forces him out of the country.

1914-1918	During World War I Albania is occupied by many different foreign powers. At the Versailles Peace Conference following the war, it is decided that Albania be allowed to remain an independent country but with no formal leaders there is chaos.
1920-1924	A group of Albanian leaders finally take control with the aid of Albanian nationalists living outside the country. Many different governments rise and fall.
1924	The conservative leader Ahmet Zogu seizes control. He rules with absolute power.
1928	Zogu declares himself king and becomes King Zog I. He prohibits any opposition but brings some stability.
1939	Italian forces invade Albania at the beginning of World War II. King Zog is forced to flee the country.
1939-1945	Throughout the war Albanian resistance to Italian occupation grows and a large underground network forms. After Italy is defeated Germany takes over occupation.
1945	Enver Hoxha, the leader of the Communist National Liberation Movement in Albania takes control of the government at the end of the war.
1945-1985	Enver Hoxha leads communist Albania for 40 years. He wields absolute power and follows a course of isolationism, separating Albania from the rest of the world.
1981	Mehmet Shehu, Hoxha's closest aid, tries to pressure him into increasing relations with other countries and is killed.

1985	Enver Hoxha dies of heart failure. Ramiz Alia, his successor, vows to keep Albania as Hoxha had wanted.
1989	Ramiz Alia allows Albanians to travel outside the country, opens the borders, and restores religious freedom.
1990	After the fall of Communism throughout Eastern Europe Alia allows political parties and elections.
1992	Multiparty elections are held and won by the Democratic Party. The Communist Socialist Party wins only 25 percent of the parliamentary seats. Sali Berisha becomes president.
1993-1996	Albania makes some economic progress and aid comes in from foreign countries and investors. Ramiz Alia and some of the Communist Socialist Party leaders are put under arrest, charged with abuse of office.
1997	The country is plunged into chaos following economic collapse caused by a pyramid investment scam. The military disband and the people take up arms. A state of emergency is declared. New elections are held and Socialist Party leader Rexhep Mejdani becomes president.
1999	Ethnic Albanians living in neighboring Kosovo flee into Albania and other bordering countries when Serbian forces invade that country killing many. Aid pours into the country to assist these refugees.
2000	Elections are held amidst accusations by the opposition Democratic Party that the ruling Socialists manipulated the polls.

1

The Struggling Albanians

During the 18th century, British historian Edward Gibbon wrote that Albania "is a country, within sight of Italy, which is less known than the interior of America." Since then, the world has come to know a great deal about America, but Albania has remained a mystery.

Situated on the west coast of the Balkan Peninsula, Albania is one of the smallest countries in Europe. It borders Serbia, Kosovo, Macedonia, Greece, and the Adriatic and Ionian seas, but impassable mountains isolate it from the rest of the continent. At its southwestern tip near the city of Vlorë, Albania is only 47 miles (75.6 kilometers) from Italy across the Strait of Otranto, a major sea passage from western and central Europe to the Near East. This access to the strait has repeatedly made the tiny nation a battleground for foreign powers seeking to control trading routes. Throughout its history, which dates from the ancient Illyrian tribes of the 3rd century B.C., Albania has endured invasion, conquest, and repression at the hands of foreign conquerors.

National hero Scanderbeg leads his Albanian countrymen in battle against the Turkish sultan in this 16th-century engraving.

For 500 years, the Ottoman (Turkish) Empire ruled Albania, giving the country a Middle Eastern flavor that further alienated it from its European neighbors. After the Communists came to power in 1945, for over 40 years Albania was a closed society. The government permitted few outsiders to enter the country, and no Albanians could leave. It allowed no foreign movies, magazines, or newspapers into the country. Since 1990 Albania's borders have been reopened and it has become a multiparty republic struggling to make up for all the time in isolation.

But even with the Albanian people so much in today's headlines due to the war over Kosovo, the Western world still knows little about the country itself. What is known is this—Albania's history is one of struggle, hardship, courage, and, most of all, survival.

Albania's rugged mountains provide an impressive backdrop for the wide-ly dispersed villages that characterize the country.

2

The Land

Albania is a land of rugged mountains, fertile valleys, and wooded uplands. Approximately the size of the state of Maryland, it covers 11,000 square miles (27,748 square kilometers). It has three geographic regions: the mountainous north, dominated by the Northern Albanian Mountains (part of the Dinaric Alps); the central region, distinguished by two large, fertile plains lying between the Mati and Vijosa rivers; and the southern region, a patchwork of mountains, plains, valleys, and rivers. *Shqiperi*, the country's traditional name in the Albanian language, means "the land of the men of the eagles," referring to the numerous eagles that nest in the Albanian mountains. Since 1991, Albania's official name has been the Republic of Albania.

The most forbidding territory is the north, where 90 percent of the land is mountainous (altogether mountains cover 70 percent of Albania). Mount Korab, the country's highest point, at 9,068 feet (2,764 meters), is located here. Snow covers Albania's northern mountains all year long. Because of the high altitude, winters are quite cold, and even summer temperatures are cool and unpredictable. A sunny summer day can turn into a chilling night in the mountain region's thick forests.

The only lake in northern Albania is Lake Shkodër, located west of the ancient city of Shkodër. Part of Lake Shkodër juts into neighboring Serbia. Northern Albania also has a few rivers although not as many as the south. The northern Drin River courses through the mountains to the town of Kukës, where it meets the Drin i zi River. The north also has one of Albania's few navigable rivers, the Buene, which flows into the Adriatic Sea. Its population of more than 47,000 makes Shkodër the third-largest city in Albania and the largest city in the northern region. Other towns in the north include Bajram Cur, Rubik, Borje, and the port city of Shengjin.

Central Albania is relatively flat, particularly toward the seacoast. The two large plains of the central region, the Kavaja and the Muzakia, are very fertile and account for most of the country's farmland (only 17.8 percent of Albania is fit for cultivation). On these plains, farmers produce much of the corn and wheat grown. The Muzakia plain is also home to a type of horse that many European cavalrymen prized during the Middle Ages.

Even though the central region is the flattest part of Albania, it has its share of mountains. The looming Mount Tomori, which, like the northern mountains, is snow-covered year-round, is visible from the Adriatic Sea. Tomori's summit, Tomoritsa, rises to 8,184 feet (2,494 meters). The second-highest peak in Albania, Gramoz, in central Albania on the Greek border, reaches 8,278 feet (2,523 meters).

The climate in the central region is generally mild, although some snow accumulates in the mountains during the relatively short Albanian winter. The average temperature in January is 42 degrees Fahrenheit (5.5 degrees Celsius), whereas in July temperatures along the coast reach 83 degrees Fahrenheit (28 degrees Celsius), much higher than those in northern Albania.

Albania's largest city, Tirana, is located in the central region. More than 240,000 people—more than 13 percent of Albania's population—live in Tirana, which is also the nation's capital. The country's second-largest population center, the port city of Durrës, is also in central Albania, on the Adriatic Sea. Durrës is the site of Albania's national weather center, the only place that reports Albania's weather conditions to the outside world.

In addition to the Mati and Vijosa rivers that mark the boundaries of central Albania, the region contains several other waterways, most notably the Seman, the Devoll, and the Shkumbi. Two large lakes make up the eastern border of central Albania—Lake Ohrid, which borders Macedonia, and Lake Prespa, which borders both Macedonia and Greece.

Southern Albania shares a border with Greece, and the Greek island of Corfu is within sight of the Albanian town of Sarandë. In contrast to the mountain regions, the southern towns along the Adriatic Sea have a mild climate, with hot, dry summers and rainy winters. The southern mountains do not reach the great heights of those in northern and central Albania. The Acroceraunian Mountains stand at roughly 4,900 feet (1,494 meters), while peaks in the Chimara range reach 6,550 feet (1,996 meters).

The southern region boasts the Bay of Vlorë, an important harbor for imports and exports. The port city of Vlorë is also the largest city in southern Albania. Another city in the region, Gjirokastër, is the birthplace of Enver Hoxha, who ruled Albania from 1946 to 1985. Although northern and central Albania are remote and isolated, southern Albania has been exposed to Western culture because it is more accessible to Greece and the rest of Europe.

Albania is subject to natural disasters. Cyclones are a threat in the coastal areas, and two major earthquakes have struck the country since the mid-1960s. In 1967, a quake measuring 6.5 on the Richter scale struck near the city of Debar on the Yugoslav border. The quake killed 20 people, injured 204, and destroyed 80 percent of the buildings in the city. A severe earthquake shook northern Albania in 1979, but because the northern mountains are sparsely populated, few injuries occurred.

Albania's population is more than 3.2 million people. But almost as many Albanians live outside the country as within it. Albania's neighbors have absorbed large numbers of Albanians who fled their country during its numerous wars and conquests. Currently, Greece and Italy, Albania's southern neighbors, are home to thousands of Albanians. Thousands of Albanians who live in neighboring Kosovo have recently suffered death and destruction at the hands of Serbians. And more than 80,000 people of Albanian ancestry live in the United States and Canada.

Albania is settled in widely dispersed villages. Only 11 Albanian towns have populations of more than 20,000, and 70

20

Because of Albania's mountainous terrain, only 30 percent of its roads are paved.

percent of the Albanian population lives in communities with fewer than 1,000 inhabitants. Although more than two-thirds of Albania's villages have electricity, automobiles are very rare. Even if more people had cars, they would not be able to use them in many places. The roads from the coastal towns to the Albanian interior are nearly impassable during winter snows and spring floods, and some mountain districts in the north are accessible only by packhorse or donkey. In some areas, the only roads are pathways that flocks of sheep and goats created as they migrated from winter pastures near the coast to summer grazing grounds in the uplands. There are only 10,400 miles (16,000 kilometers) of roadway in Albania, and only 30 percent are paved. Many rural settlements are 10 miles (16 kilometers) or more from the nearest road. Although many of the roads are well-constructed, they frequently need repair due to the harsh climate in the mountain areas. Furthermore, road construction is very expensive. Roads must be engineered around mountains, and bridges must be built over the country's many rivers.

The country has a total of 435 miles (670 kilometers) of railroad. The main railway is 18 miles (29 kilometers) long and connects the capital, Tirana, with the port city of Durrës. There is also a one-track railroad from Durrës to the inland city of Elbasan, south of Tirana. But few Albanians travel by train, and Albania's railroads most often serve commercial purposes. Albania has nine airports with the major international one in Tirana. There is air service to all the major European cities.

An Albanian surveys damage caused by one of the earthquakes to which the country is subject.

3

A History of Turbulence and Survival

Albania bears the traces of a turbulent past. Since ancient times, neighboring powers have invaded the country, trying to gain control of its strategic ports and shipping lanes. At one time or another, Greeks, Romans, Goths, Byzantines, Serbs, Bulgarians, Italians, and Turks have held Albania.

Present-day Albania was known in ancient times as Illyria. In fact, the Albanian people are direct descendants of the Illyrian tribes who formed a kingdom in the Balkan Peninsula around 300 B.C. Albanian clan life, which continues to be the mainstay of traditional Albanian society, is based on the principles of self-governing Illyrian communities.

The most famous Illyrian leader, King Argon, ruled during the second half of the 3rd century B.C. and united the many Illyrian tribes to create a powerful nation. Under his rule, the Illyrians developed a highly advanced society that had a sophisticated system of government and exported goods to neighboring countries.

Ruins of this amphitheater form a monument to the Roman Empire, which controlled the kingdom of Illyria for more than 200 years.

Argon was also a powerful military leader. Illyria's strong army was fierce in battle, and its navy bravely defended the peninsula from seaborne invasion. The last capital of Illyria was Scodra, known today as the northern Albanian city of Shkodër.

After King Argon's death in 231 B.C., the power of the Illyrian kingdom began to wane. Because of its strategic access to the Strait of Otranto and the Adriatic shipping lanes, many other powers tried to gain control of Illyria. In 167 B.C., the Illyrians fell to the Roman Empire.

The Romans allowed the Illyrian tribes to rule themselves but forced them to pledge their allegiance to the emperor. Eventually,

24

Illyria and its people became an integral part of the empire, and because of their skill on the battlefield, Illyrian warriors became favorites of the Roman emperors. Many Illyrian soldiers rose to great power. Several of Rome's strongest emperors—Claudius II Gothicus, Aurelian, Diocletian, Constantine the Great—were Illyrians who gained power through their military prowess.

In 395 A.D., the Roman Empire fell, and Illyria became part of Byzantium, the great Eastern empire centered in what is now Istanbul, Turkey. Between the third and fifth centuries, Illyria was overrun by Huns and Visigoths, warriors from the neighboring Slavic territories. Great numbers of Slavic peoples began to immigrate to the Illyrian territory. By the end of the seventh century, the Slavic culture had absorbed most of the Illyrian tribes. The

The church of St. Mary at Apollonia reveals Byzantine influence.

only area where Illyrians retained their nationality and language was in the region known today as Albania.

For several centuries, Albania was divided into a number of feudal states (parcels of land ruled by noble families). In the 14th century, the Serbian king Stephen Dushan took over much of Albania and incorporated it into his empire. After King Stephen's death in 1355, however, the Albanian feudal families regained control of their lands. These powerful families quarreled constantly and by the turn of the century, a full-scale territorial war had erupted. One of the groups involved in this dispute turned to the Turkish Empire for assistance. But instead of securing the rights of the feudal rulers, the Turks used this opportunity to overrun Albanian territories. By 1430, they had gained power over all of Albania.

Albania's once powerful feudal lords became vassals of the Turkish sultan. The sultan ordered them to prove their loyalty to the Turkish Empire by giving him their sons. The Turks, who were Muslims, raised these Albanian boys in the Islamic faith and gave them extensive military training. The rulers gave Albanian Muslims privileged status. They considered those who had converted to Islam to be Turks and permitted them to enjoy the benefits of that title (they labeled Orthodox Christians "Greeks," and called Catholics "Latins"). Muslims entered the sultan's service as *arnauts*, soldiers who formed the backbone of the Turkish army. The sultan appointed a number of Albanians to the post of grand *vizier* (a high ranking official of the Turkish administration) and selected his personal bodyguard and the special garrison at Constantinople (the capital of the empire) from the ranks of Albanian soldiers. These circumstances determined the career of Albania's greatest national hero, known to the Western world as Scanderbeg.

Scanderbeg, born Gjergj Kastrioti in 1405, was the son of a wealthy Albanian lord. When Kastrioti was very young, the Turks took him from his family, as they took other sons of feudal

Almost every Albanian town boasts a statue of hero Scanderbeg.

lords, and brought him to the sultan's palace in Constantinople, where he received an education and military training and converted from Christianity to Islam.

Kastrioti served as a soldier for the Turkish Empire and took part in military expeditions in both Asia Minor and Europe.

This fresco commemorates Scanderbeg's visit to Pope Nicholas V, who dubbed the Albanian the "Champion of Christendom."

Under Turkish rule, most Albanians converted to Islam.

Brave and fierce in battle, he rose quickly through the ranks. Soon, he became an officer and distinguished himself as one of the sultan's ablest commanders. The sultan awarded him one of the greatest military honors in the empire—the title "Skander Bey," Turkish for "Lord Alexander" (a reference to Alexander the Great). Over time, "Skander Bey" became "Scanderbeg."

Scanderbeg would eventually use against their empire the military training he received from the Turks. In 1443, he returned to his homeland, where he publicly renounced Islam and declared a holy war against the Turks. The Albanian people united with Scanderbeg to fight the empire, and the Roman Catholic Church lent its support to their efforts. Pope Nicholas V called Scanderbeg the "Champion of Christendom."

Although his troops were ill-trained and greatly outnumbered, Scanderbeg managed to liberate most of Albania. For more than a quarter of a century, the Albanians stalled Turkish advances. After Scanderbeg's death in 1468, however, resistance to the Turks waned. By 1478, the sultanate had again gained control of Albania. Nonetheless, Scanderbeg remains the symbol of freedom and independence for all Albanians. Today, almost every Albanian town has a statue of Scanderbeg, and the red standard with the double-headed eagle that he raised as his banner of revolt is still the country's flag.

The Turks ruled Albania for almost 500 years, keeping the country isolated from the mainstream of Western civilization. The Turkish Empire ruled Albania with an iron fist. In addition to raising Albanian boys to be Turkish warriors, it confiscated the land and property of anyone who did not embrace Islam. Most Albanians, given the choice between sacrificing their land and weaponry and relinquishing their Christianity, converted to Islam. An old Albanian proverb expressed their reasoning well: "The creed follows the sword." Christianity survived only in the mountainous north and the extreme south of Albania, where the Turks were unable to penetrate. When Albania gained its independence from Turkey in 1912, approximately 70 percent of the population was Muslim, 20 percent (almost exclusively in the southern area bordering on Greece) was Greek Orthodox, and 10 percent (concentrated in the north) was Roman Catholic.

The Turks also gave Muslims ruling power. By the 18th century, Albania was divided into *cifliks* (hereditary estates) controlled by Muslim landlords and cultivated by tenant farmers. Each ciflik was ruled by a *bey,* or native chief. Although the beys were officially vassals of the sultan, they ruled their territories as independent princes. The beys were jealous of and hostile to one another, and they frequently fought over land. The Turks encouraged this infighting. It was much easier for them to retain control over a weak, fragmented territory than over a strong, unified nation.

Nonetheless, a few powerful Albanian leaders emerged during this period. The most influential was Ali Pasha of Janina, who dominated southern and central Albania from 1788 until 1822. Although the sultan considered him a servant of the Ottoman Empire, Ali Pasha actually had more power over the Albanian territory than the Turkish leader did. In fact, Ali Pasha secretly lent his support to revolts against Turkish rule. British poet George Gordon, Lord Byron, mentioned Ali Pasha in his famous poem *Childe Harold's Pilgrimage*, which he wrote after meeting Ali Pasha during a trip to Albania in the early 1800s.

Around the same time, between 1757 and 1822, the Bushati clan, a powerful family, ruled northern Albania. The Bushati patriarch, Mehmet Bushati (1760-1831), led many revolts against Turkish rule, but his forces were no match for the empire's arnauts. Although the Bushatis and Ali Pasha remained powerful in their respective regions, neither was able to gain control of all of Albania. Because there was no leader to unify the country, Albania remained divided.

4

The Rise of Nationalism

Eventually, the forces of nationalism (the desire for an independent, unified country) began to tear at the Turkish Empire. The various nations under Turkish rule wanted independence, and their people entertained thoughts of rebellion. Throughout the 18th and 19th centuries, almost every European observer felt that Turkish strength was decaying so rapidly that the Turkish presence in Europe could not last much longer. Even French emperor Napoleon Bonaparte recognized that the Turkish Empire was faltering. In the 1790s, he noted: "It is of no use to try to maintain the Turkish Empire; we shall witness its fall in our time." During the War of Greek Independence (1821), Britain's Duke of Wellington believed the empire's end was at hand, and in 1853, the Czar of Russia told the English ambassador: "We have a sick man on our hands and must prepare for his demise." For some time after, Turkey was called "the sick man of Europe."

By the mid-19th century, an independence movement had begun to take hold in Albania. In 1880, Albanian nationalist

Scanderbeg's coat of arms appears on Albania's flag.

groups and newspapers aimed at fostering patriotism and gaining foreign support for an autonomous Albanian state began to appear in Europe and the United States. In 1908, the Albanians revolted. After four years of sporadic fighting, the Turkish government agreed to create an independent country. On November 28, 1912, a national assembly of Albanian notables led by Ismail Kemal Bey Vlora proclaimed independence.

Vlora, a deputy in the Turkish parliament and a noted Albanian political leader, headed the provisional government. On July 29, 1913, the European Conference of Ambassadors (a meeting of the representatives of many European nations) confirmed Albania's independence. But the European community was concerned

33

about the stability of the provisional government. The Albanian people had little experience in governing themselves. The country had never held elections. The only Albanians with any administrative experience were beys, such as Vlora, who were known for disputes among themselves and were distrusted by many Albanians because of their previous loyalty to the Turks.

In an attempt to create a more stable government, the ambassadors decreed that Albania should be a hereditary monarchy and that a member of a European royal family should be chosen to be the new Albanian sovereign. They soon selected a German prince, William of Wied.

William of Wied arrived in his new kingdom on March 1914. Albanians were less than delighted with their new monarch. Some Albanians felt that the European ambassadors had little right to choose a government for Albania, much less to declare a German prince the Albanian king. Essad Pasha, a powerful feudal leader, mounted a rebellion against the new monarchy. Within six months, the rebels forced William of Wied to flee the country, and Essad Pasha became the Albanian head of state.

An Albanian boy shoulders his rolled-up, portable bed, made from a three-ply straw mat.

An Albanian shepherd takes a break from his labors to draw on his pipe.

Unfortunately for Albania, however, when the hour of liberation arrived, so did World War I. The country became a battlefield as the armies of Serbia, Greece, Italy, France, and the Austro-Hungarian Empire fought to control it. As the war dragged on, first one and then another foreign group dominated Albania. Essad Pasha's government collapsed.

In 1919, after the end of the war, Greece, Yugoslavia, and Italy wanted to divide Albania among themselves. But Albania was not partitioned. At the Versailles Peace Conference (a postwar meeting between the leaders of the nations involved in World War I), United States President Woodrow Wilson personally intervened on behalf of an independent Albania. He fought for an international agreement to guarantee the borders of the country. Within those borders, however, there was chaos.

On January 21, 1920, a group of prominent Albanians drew up a constitution. For the next four years, the people enjoyed the greatest amount of political freedom in their history—Albanians finally ran Albania. The creation of this independent Albanian

35

state was largely the work of Albanian nationalists living outside of the country. Indispensable aid came from patriotic centers in Romania, Bulgaria, and Egypt. Albanians roamed from one Near Eastern capital to another seeking support for their cause. But many of these countries did not want foreign nationals stirring up trouble within their borders. For help in creating a democratic state, Albanians turned to the United States.

Only in the United States could Albanian nationalists establish a permanent movement. Americans of Albanian descent who pas-

Albanian Americans celebrate Albanian Flag Day by wearing the Tosk kilt, or *fustanella*.

sionately wanted to see democracy established in their homeland contributed money to the independence movement. The Albanians spent whatever political energy or idealism they had in the fight for an independent, democratic Albania.

Albanian immigrants to America seldom interacted with other Americans. These immigrants, especially the first generation, had an insatiable desire to help countrymen who followed them to the land of freedom. Following Albanian custom, the *konak* or coffeehouse, was the nucleus of social life. In the cities of Massachusetts where many Albanians settled, people gathered in these konaks to discuss events in the mother country. In large, smoky rooms, they gossiped about the latest news from their hometowns. Newly arrived immigrants brought personal messages from loved ones. Albanian newspapers lay about. The coffeehouse became the Albanian immigrant's employment agency as well as his political forum and social club, providing job information for newcomers. Above all, the coffeehouse served as the place to debate the rapidly changing circumstances in Albania.

The Albanians who immigrated to the United States deeply affected events in Albania. American ideas about democracy and freedom helped bring about the 1908 uprising that was the first step in ending Turkish rule. After the Turks were ousted, many Albanian Americans returned to their homeland with stacks of books, newspapers, and magazines in the Albanian language, which the Turks had outlawed in 1902. Returning immigrants also brought other Western wonders to Albania. When they brought the first phonograph into the Albanian interior, country people were initially terrified and then delighted by the newfangled music machine. The Western clothing of Albanians who had returned to their homeland from America inspired native Albanians to imitate them. Before long, American styles appeared in the crooked lanes of inland villages.

Albanians who remained in America sent money to their homeland to improve peasant lands and make houses more habitable. In Boston and Worcester, Massachusetts, local groups raised money to finance construction in Albanian towns. Soon, Albanian American money turned into bridges, roads, schools, and town halls.

It seemed for a time that American influence would transform the independent Albania created in 1920. Scores of Albanian Americans returned to their homeland and became government officials, deputies, police commissioners, army officers, and

American philanthropist Charles R. Crane generously supported the first Albanian public school system in the 1930s.

schoolteachers. The American Junior Red Cross raised funds to finance the American Technical School of Tirana. This school, in operation until 1933, educated hundreds of Albanian boys in simple technology. American money also funded the first Albanian public school system. Charles R. Crane, a Chicago philanthropist who had made a fortune selling bathroom fixtures, generously supported this pioneering education work. Engineers paid by contributions from Americans built the first electric plant in Tirana. A weekly newspaper, *Shqipetar i Amerikes* (The Albanian American), spread the doctrine of democracy and encouraged the people to participate in government. Many Albanian Americans enthusiastically believed that democracy could take hold in their homeland and that they could help build a mini-United States in southeastern Europe.

The peaceful, democratic state hoped for by Albanian Americans was not to be. Instead, political turmoil overwhelmed the Albanian government. Although the political leaders—largely officials of the old Turkish bureaucracy—attempted to lay the foundations of a modern state, a bitter struggle between conservative landowners and western-educated liberals prevented this. Led by Ahmet Zogu, a member of one of the country's wealthiest families, the landowners advocated continuing the semifeudal land system. They opposed social and economic reforms, especially in agriculture. The liberals favored the immediate creation of a Western-style democracy. The liberal leader was Bishop Fan S. Noli, a graduate of Harvard College who had founded the

Albanian Autocephalous Orthodox Church in Boston in 1908 and returned to Albania in 1920.

Neither the liberals nor the conservatives could obtain a clear mandate to govern. Governments rose and fell with alarming frequency. Noli wanted sweeping economic and social reforms, while Zogu urged restraint and conservatism in formulating programs. The conservatives gained control of the government in 1923, but pro-Noli revolutionaries overthrew them in June 1924 and forced Zogu to flee to Yugoslavia.

The liberals then installed Bishop Noli as chief executive of the Albanian government. Noli immediately proposed agrarian changes that would have dramatically altered the prevailing landholding system. He made bold moves in the area of foreign policy as well, such as officially recognizing the Soviet Union—a decision that alienated many of his supporters both at home and in the United States.

But after he had been in office for six months, it was clear that Noli could not carry out many of his ambitious programs. In December of 1924, Zogu seized power, aided by Yugoslavia and by British oil interests (who thought there might be untapped oil in southern Albania and wanted exclusive oil leases). Bishop Noli and his closest aids fled to the United States. Other Noli supporters went to Moscow in the Soviet Union or joined Communist parties in other Eastern European capitals.

The attempt to create a Western-style democracy in Albania was a dismal failure. Under Zogu, personal feuds, shootings in the new assembly, and confusion in public administration combined to defeat efforts to bring about law and order. Zogu wielded absolute power and ruled Albania as a virtual president-dictator from December 1924 until 1928. On September 1, 1928, he had himself crowned king and transformed Albania into a hereditary monarchy. From that moment on, he was known as Zog I, king of the Albanians.

Zog's reign brought political stability to the country. Zog squelched political dissent by prohibiting political parties. Attempts to overthrow him in 1932, 1935, and 1937, were unsuccessful. Even though he had absolute power, Zog ruled as a moderate dictator.

Although he made no sweeping reforms, Zog did outlaw the traditional vendetta, or blood feud, which until that time accounted for one out of four male deaths in Albania. He also took steps to introduce a national education system and started modest public works programs. Above all, Zog's 14-year rule—the longest span

King Zog, shown here with his sisters, ruled Albania for 14 years.

King Zog with his bride, Countess Geraldine Apponyi of Hungary.

of an Albanian government since Scanderbeg—saw the development of an Albanian national consciousness. Albanians, so long divided and ruled by foreigners, could now identify with their nation, even if they felt no loyalty to the monarchy.

During Zog's reign, Albania began to involve itself in the world community. Zog concluded several military and economic treaties with Italy, led by Premier Benito Mussolini. Relations between the neighboring nations seemed almost friendly. In fact, the Italian foreign minister, Count Galeazzo Ciano, served as best man at Zog's 1938 wedding to Geraldine Apponyi (a Hungarian countess whose mother was American). Then, on April 7, 1939 Italian forces invaded Albania. Within one week, the independent state collapsed. Zog's meager and poorly trained army proved no match for the Italian war machine. Italy quickly placed Albania under the crown of King Victor Emanuel II and imposed a fascist regime, forcing Zog and his family to flee the country.

42

As 1939 drew to a close, all of Europe became engulfed in World War II. Italy joined with Adolf Hitler's Germany in the war against the Allies (Great Britain, France, and the United States). The Albanians did not want to fight for their foreign occupier, and resistance to Italian occupation grew. As the Allies gradually began to defeat Mussolini's fascist state, Albanian partisan forces increased in strength. At the end of 1942, resistance fighters numbered between 8,000 and 10,000. By the summer of 1943, when the Italian war effort collapsed, resistance groups occupied almost all of Albania.

In January 1944, the German army moved into Albania, decisively defeating the partisan forces. Instead of squelching the resistance movement, however, the German invasion fueled the fire of independence. At the end of 1944, Albanian fighters totaled about 70,000 and had incurred more than 28,000 casualties in the fight for freedom. As the Allies beat Germany into submission, Albania's Communist-controlled National Liberation Movement, led by Enver Hoxha (pronounced enn-VEHR HAW-dja), strengthened its hold over various partisan groups. At the end of the war, Hoxha became the head of the Communist government that took over Albania.

King Zog died in exile, and Queen Geraldine and her son, Zog II, fled to Paris to await the overthrow of the Communist government. Many Albanian anti-Communists rallied around Zog II, and he became the leader of those opposed to Communist rule.

5

Enver Hoxha

Enver Hoxha, for 40 years the leader of Communist Albania, was born on October 16, 1908, in Gjirokastër, a market town in southern Albania. His father was a Muslim cloth merchant. When Hoxha was in his teens, his father sent him to a French-run secondary school in Korce in eastern Albania, where he developed his writing skills. After secondary school, Hoxha received a scholarship to study at the University of Montpelier in France.

Hoxha went to Montpelier, but he was expelled a year later for "neglect of work." After his expulsion he went to Paris, where he began to associate with a small group of Albanian Communists living in exile. Hoxha used his writing skills to pen articles for the French Communist newspaper *L'Humanité* (Humanity).

In 1934, Hoxha went to Brussels, Belgium, to become a secretary to the Albanian consul. He also studied law at a local university and continued to write for *L'Humanité*. The articles he wrote criticized the Albanian monarchy of King Zog, and as a result, the consul canceled his appointment. In 1936, Hoxha

Triumphant Italian soldiers drive through Tirana's streets in 1939.

returned to Albania, where he continued his attacks on the government while working as a French teacher, first in Tirana and later at his old school in Korce. In 1939, he went to jail for his anti-government statements.

Later that year, the Italian army conquered Albania. When the new Italian-run government declared war against Great Britain and France in 1940, Hoxha went underground. In 1941, he founded the Albanian Communist Party and became editor of the party newspaper.

Hoxha's outlawed party operated secretly out of a tobacco shop in Tirana. When the Italians closed in on the shop, Hoxha fled to the mountains. With aid from American and British personnel, as well as from Soviet military officers who had parachuted into

45

Albania, the former French teacher built a guerrilla force of about 70,000 fighters, who continued to battle the Italians and fought the German forces that invaded Albania later in the war.

After Italy surrendered in 1944, its forces withdrew from Albania. In October 1944, the Communist guerrillas proclaimed a provisional government. Their leader, General Enver Hoxha, became prime minister and defense minister. In 1945, the Western Allies agreed to recognize the new government, on the condition that Hoxha would soon hold free and democratic elections.

When balloting took place later that year, however, only one list of candidates appeared—those sponsored by the Communist Party. Hoxha was declared Albania's ruler, and he promptly proclaimed a People's Republic. The United States and Great Britain immediately revoked their recognition of his government.

Hoxha wielded absolute power. Through fear and intimidation, he managed to eliminate virtually all Albanians who opposed his rigid government. Anyone who dared to question Hoxha's policies risked being thrown into prison and forgotten. Even those

Albanians and Italians alike crowd the capital city's streets during the Italian occupation.

who agreed with him lived in fear of plots against them. Hoxha also persecuted ethnic minorities in Albania, especially the Greeks. His primary target, however, was religion.

The Hoxha government outlawed all public worship in 1947. In 1967, the government declared that the only religion for an Albania must be "Albanianism." Enver Hoxha personally called upon the youth of the nation to take the lead in the antireligious mission. By May of 1967, religious groups had turned over to the government some 2,300 churches, mosques, cloisters, and shrines, most of which were converted into cultural centers for young people. Hoxha's plan to create the first atheist nation in the world proceeded rapidly.

According to the few Western reporters who were in Tirana in 1967, Communist officials seized churches, mosques, and monasteries by going from village to village, intimidating villagers into requesting permission to close their holy places. Stating that it supported the will of the people, the government issued orders to close the houses of worship.

When members of the clergy opposed the decree, the government took drastic measures. The strongest resistance came from the Catholic clergy. To intimidate the clergy and prevent further opposition, the government burned down the Franciscan cloister in Shkodër in the spring of 1967, killing four monks. The government also removed the ornate facade from the Catholic cathedral in Tirana and converted the building into a people's museum. The Catholic cathedrals in Shkodër and Durrës suffered a similar fate.

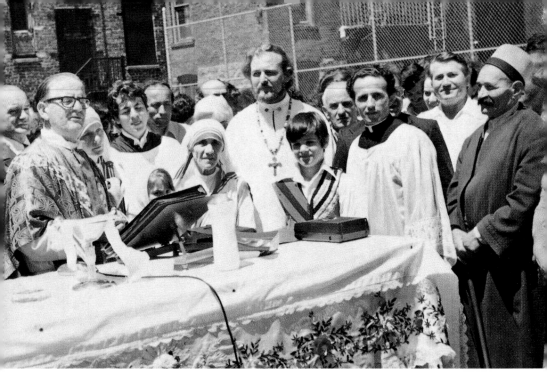

Albanian Americans of three faiths—Albanian Orthodox, Roman Catholic, and Islam—gather in Boston to greet Mother Teresa, whose parents were Albanian.

After it seized a house of worship, the government forced the younger clergymen to work either in industry or in agriculture collectives. It ordered the elder clergy back to their birthplaces, which they could not leave without permission from the authorities. The leader of Albania's Catholics, Monsignor Ernest Coba, had to seek work as a gardener on a collective farm.

Throughout the 1970s, Communist leaders continued to call for an intensified struggle against religion. They especially strove to eradicate the religious beliefs of students and young people who remained under the influence of their parents. Just as the Turks had worked to change the religious nature of Albania, so the Communists sought to alter Albanian religious life. Although some Albanians still practiced their religion, they had to do so secretly. In 1980, one international agency estimated the religious makeup of Albania as 20.5 percent Muslim, 18.7 percent atheist, 5.4 percent Christian, and 55.4 percent "nonreligious."

Hoxha was an admirer of the Soviet leader Joseph Stalin and sought to emulate Stalin's government by instituting Soviet policies in Albania. But Hoxha was not as powerful as Stalin. Hoxha supported the Soviet Union's 1948 break with Yugoslavia, but then, fearing retaliation from Yugoslavia, he cut all ties with that

Soviet leader Joseph Stalin greatly influenced Enver Hoxha.

country and expelled Yugoslav Communists who had assisted the Albanian guerrillas.

When Stalin died in 1953, Nikita Khrushchev became the leader of the Soviet Union. In 1955, Khrushchev restored relations with Yugoslavia. This move threatened Hoxha, and he purged his government of associates who supported Khrushchev. When the Soviet Union launched the Sputnik space program in 1957, an angry Hoxha called the rocket an imperialist weapon and a threat to world peace.

In 1961, Khrushchev denounced the Stalin government for its extreme repressiveness and abusiveness. Hoxha, still an ardent admirer of the late Stalin, promptly broke off relations with the Soviet Union. From then on, his only remaining foreign friend, the Communist People's Republic of China, supplied Albania with needed economic and technical assistance. In 1972, however,

Hoxha speaks before members of the Albanian People's Assembly.

Chinese-American relations improved. Hoxha grew disillusioned with Red China, and their once cordial relations chilled.

In the late 1970s, some members of Albania's Politburo (the governing body of the Communist Party) began to push for increased relations with the outside world. Hoxha would not hear of it. In 1981, Mehmet Shehu, for 40 years Hoxha's closest aide and the number two man in the Politburo, made the mistake of pressuring Hoxha to increase foreign relations during a central committee meeting. The next day, Shehu's death was announced. Although Albanian authorities labeled his death a suicide, it is believed that Hoxha took out a pistol and shot Shehu dead on the floor of the assembly. In 1985, the official Albanian news agency announced that Shehu had indeed been "liquidated" because his views were a danger to the Albanian people.

The killing of a French woman who was vacationing on the Greek island of Corfu, located a few miles off the coast of southern Albania, provided further evidence of Hoxha's fear of the outside world. Border guards shot and killed her when they felt she and her scuba diving group came too close to the Albanian shoreline. As a result, France promptly recalled its Albanian ambassador and severed all diplomatic relations with Hoxha's government.

Eventually, however, Hoxha began to realize the need for improved relations with other countries. In 1984, he secured trade agreements with Italy, Greece, Turkey, and Austria. In January 1985, Albania reopened the main highway linking Greece to the Greek-inhabited areas of southern Albania. (The highway closed in 1940 when Italy used it to invade Greece from occupied Albania.) The two countries hoped that reopening this highway would improve relations between them and permit greater contact between Greece and the 200,000 Greeks living in Albania's south. Also in 1985, Greece renounced all territorial claims to southern Albania and ended the 44-year-old official state of war that had existed between the two countries since World War II. With this gesture, Greece hoped to reduce the persecution of Albania's Greek minority.

In turn, Albania made a gesture toward Greece. The government offered to return a Greek funeral urn from a ruined monastery in the town of Kolikandasi on the Zeman River, near Berat. The urn allegedly contained the remains of Kosma the Aetolian, a Greek saint who was murdered in Albania in 1779. The transfer never took place, however. The Greek Orthodox Church requires that a church official supervise any transfer of relics, but because the Albanian government closed all churches in 1967, there were no officials in Albania to perform the service. And the government would not allow a foreign church official to enter the country.

On April 11, 1985, Enver Hoxha died of heart failure. When the Soviet Union sent a message of condolence to the Albanian embassy in Vienna, the message was returned. "We'll have nothing to do with [the Soviets]," the Albanian ambassador said. Albania accepted the sympathy of Communist China, but barred all foreign diplomats from the funeral. At services for Hoxha held in Scanderbeg Square, new Albanian leader Ramiz Alia eulogized

Albanian leader Enver Hoxha casts his ballot in the 1967 national elections.

Hoxha. He vowed to keep Albania "always strong, always Red, as [Hoxha] wanted it."

For 40 years, Hoxha had ruled Albania with an iron fist. His autobiography, which includes his speeches and reminiscences, is more than 40 volumes long. Its theme is that capitalism enslaves the masses and that Communism is the only just socioeconomics system. Perhaps the only way to understand the philosophy of Enver Hoxha is through his own words, written in 1982:

Both the bitter history of our country in the past and the reality of the "world" that they advertise have convinced us that it is by no means a "civilized world" but a world in which the bigger and stronger oppress and flay the smaller and weaker, in which money and corruption make the law, and injustice, perfidy, and backstabbing triumph.

Ramiz Alia eventually realized that if the country was to improve its economic situation it must open its borders and allow contact with the international community. In 1989 with the winds of change in the air he allowed for Albanians to travel outside the country, allowed foreign investment and aid into the country, restored religious freedom, and started allowing some forms of free-market economy. After the fall of Communism throughout Eastern Europe in that same year, great pressure was placed to allow political parties and elections. Finally in 1992 a multiparty election was held and the Democratic Party won a majority of the parliamentary seats. The Communist Socialist Party only took 25 percent of the seats. Sali Berisha became the new republic's president.

Over the next four years Albania's economy improved slightly but the years of isolation had taken their toll. Some foreign aid and investments helped to improve conditions. Businesses were privatized–no longer owned by the state.

Then in 1997 the economy collapsed after a pyramid investment scam left one out of every three Albanians penniless. Riots followed and the military disbanded. The United Nations sent in a peacekeeping force to bring order and help to distribute humanitarian aid to the suffering populace. Elections were held toward the end of the year and the Socialist Party leader, Rexhep Mejdani became president. The country was in bankruptcy, many of its factories closed, and the basic necessities were scarce.

In 1999 the struggling republic was devastated when Albanians living in neighboring Kosovo were killed or exiled by Serbian troops trying to retain the province of Kosovo under Serb rule. Many of them fled to their native Albania seeking asylum. Relief organizations sent aid to care for the thousands of refugees crossing the borders out of Kosovo into Albania and other bordering countries.

Wearing full military dress, soldiers of the Royal Albanian Guard pledge allegiance to the king of Italy in 1939.

6

The Albanian People

Whereas the populations of most nations include people from many different national and cultural backgrounds, 98 percent of Albanians are Albanian in national origin and speech. They are descendants of the Albanoi, the only Illyrian tribe that was able to resist Slavic absorption. The Albanian people are divided into two groups: the Ghegs, who live in the mountain regions north of the Shkumbi River, and the Tosks, who live south of the river, mainly in the lowlands and the plains. The rough Albanian terrain separates these two groups from one another. Because the interior of the country is rugged and many of the rivers are not navigable, northern and southern Albania conducted trade by sea until the 20th century. The great distance that separated the Ghegs and the Tosks, the limited contact between them, and the difference in climate and lifestyle between the north and south have led to many cultural differences.

The Ghegs of northern Albania comprise 67 percent of the population. They are taller than the Tosks, and the name "Gheg" is

These Albanian Americans wear costumes native to Ghegs and Tosks.

believed to be derived from the Greek *gigas*, meaning "giant."
Ghegs have long faces and curved, high-bridged noses. Before the
Communist government outlawed religion, most Ghegs followed
the Sunni Muslim faith, although some were Roman Catholic.
Because the majority of them live in the isolated north, Ghegs
have held fast to their feudal land system and ancient customs.
Even today, they are not as Westernized as Tosks.

The Tosk people are shorter and have rounder faces and smaller
noses than the Ghegs. Because they live in the accessible south,
Tosks have borne the brunt of the numerous invasions of their
country. As a result, they are more European in outlook and cus-

58

tom than the Ghegs. Until 1945, most Tosks were peasants. Almost all of the Albanians who immigrated to the United States in the late 19th and early 20th centuries were Tosk peasants in search of a better life. Many Tosks also immigrated to northern Greece. Like the Ghegs, most Tosks were traditionally Muslim, although Muslim Tosks were evenly divided between the Sunni and Bektashi sects. In addition, a substantial minority of Tosks were Christians who followed the Albanian Orthodox religion.

Although Ghegs and Tosks both speak the Albanian language, they pronounce it differently. Gheg speech has a nasal quality, and its words and phrases are short and clipped. Ghegs speak more forcefully than Tosks, and their speech is full of inflections.

Traditional garb includes richly embroidered clothing.

The Tosks do not use as much accent or inflection when they speak. Their speech is plain and smooth, and more monotonous. Although Tosks and Ghegs can usually understand one another—much as people from the northern and southern United States can comprehend each other—some Ghegs from the most remote regions of the north cannot converse with Tosks from the extreme south.

Traditionally, Albanian society was made up of *barjaks*, or clans. A barjak was a collection of *fis* (families) who lived and worked as a group. Each barjak had a leader, known as a *baryaktar* (banner bearer), who was responsible for the welfare of the clan.

The clan demanded total loyalty and obedience from all of its members. Each clan had common land and possessions that it divided among the members on the basis of need. Property was considered not "mine" but "ours." If another tribe attempted to take over a clan's territory, all clan members were expected to band together to defend their land. Just as clansmen had an obligation to their barjak, so the barjak had an obligation to its members. If a clan member became ill or injured, or suffered some material loss (such as the burning down of his house), everyone in the clan had a sacred obligation to assist the unfortunate clansman.

Because clan members jointly owned all property, they decided by committee how to divide it. If a clan member wanted a piece of property or needed a tool or some other community possession, he would call a tribal meeting. The baryaktar would head the meeting, which the leader of each fis, usually the eldest male, would attend. These men would vote to decide whether the clan member should receive what he had asked for. Petitioners presented special cases before the *pleqet* or *pleqnija*, the tribal supreme court. The pleqet consisted of the most respected elders of the community. The decision of the tribal court was final, and all clan members had to abide by it.

If a clansman violated tribal law or went against the decision of the tribal court, he risked being ostracized by the clan or being forced off tribal lands. The clan had the right to burn down a violator's house and expel him from the tribe. In extreme cases, the baryaktar could order that a violator be executed for his crimes against the tribe. "Justice is strong when the clan is strong," claims an ancient tribal motto.

In the event of a dispute between two different clans, the baryaktars of the clans would meet. Often the chief of a third clan would be present as a mediator. The chiefs would settle disputes between clans by referring to an unwritten code of laws known as the *Canon of Lek*, named after Leka Dukagjini, a powerful baryaktar of ancient times. The *Canon of Lek* contained statutory, crimi-

Leka Dukagjini compiled and gave his name to the *Canon of Lek*, an ancient code of laws.

This couple displays folk costumes from the Gjirocastër region.

nal, civil, and family laws, as well as rules for criminal and civil court proceedings. All tribes abided by it. Until the 20th century, baryaktars settled many Albanian disputes according to the ancient laws of the Canon. In 1933, a Franciscan monk named Shtjefen Gjecovi wrote down the first Albanian-language version of the Canon. Although the present court system does not use the Canon, many Albanians cherish their copy of the ancient rule book.

Honor was the ultimate virtue in the Albanian clan culture. The most important tribal institution was the *bessa*, or word of honor. Once a member gave a bessa, he could not revoke it. If a clansman went back on his bessa, his tribe ostracized him and he became the victim of universal contempt. If a tribesman gave his bessa to a member of another tribe, he was responsible to both clans if he reneged.

Another aspect of clan life was the *gyak*, or blood feud. If a clansman killed a member of another clan, the nearest male relative of the victim was honor-bound to avenge the death by killing the murderer or a member of his clan. A number of rules governed blood feuds. Victims could not be women, children, or

Departing from tradition, Albanian women receive equal treatment in society.

priests. If there were no adult male clansmen upon whom the death could be avenged, the avenger could wait until the male children of the violating clan were old enough to be killed.

Sometimes, gyaks lasted for generations. Because of the constant threat of blood reprisals, many Albanian families lived in large, impenetrable stone forts and made friendships only with people from clans who lived in another town or sector of the country. They believed that if their friends lived far away from them, they would be less likely to interfere in their affairs and start blood feuds.

Traditionally, members of the same clan did not marry. Members of different clans married one another in order to bind clans together and preserve the strength of the Albanian community. Often, the baryaktar arranged marriages according to what would be most advantageous to the clan, choosing brides based on the power and reputation of their families. Because Albanians believed that children would resemble their maternal uncles, the baryaktar would consider the appearance of a woman's brothers before selecting her as a mate for a tribesman.

Within each fis, respect for parental authority was a dominant value. Children learned to respect their elders, especially their father, whose word was law. Upon the death of the father, authority passed to the oldest male of the family. Women, with the exception of the mother, occupied an inferior position. When the time came for sons to set up their own households, they divided all of their parents' property equally among themselves. Daughters did not share in this distribution of wealth unless they had no brothers and never married.

Although the authority of the family patriarch has diminished somewhat since the end of World War II, traditional values still prevail in the countryside, especially in the mountains. Many Albanians still follow ancient traditions of courtship, such as the arranged marriage, although some young Albanians are rebelling against arranged marriages.

Albanians arrange marriages in many ways. While she is an infant, a girl may be engaged to marry a certain man when she reaches adulthood. A young male may go to an intermediary and relate his desire for a particular young woman. Or, a father may ask an intermediary to find a suitable young man for his daughter. When both sets of parents have consulted and agreed upon a match, they ask the young man and woman to give their consent. Most Albanians do not refuse a marriage their parents have arranged. If a girl in northern Albania refuses an arranged match she must vow perpetual chastity. Girls in southern Albania who refuse to marry the man their parents choose may not marry any other man in their hometown.

After arranging a match, parents plan an elaborate wedding celebration. Usually, both families hold separate festivals, inviting their own guests and bearing their own expenses. Wedding parties almost always start on Saturday night, when guests gather around long tables laden with food and drink. The wedding guests sing Albanian folk songs and dance until dawn.

An Albanian bride receives a *dunti* (hope chest) from her hus-

For a woman, traditional dress includes trousers gathered at the ankles and a gold-embroidered vest.

band's family. Inside the dunti are a variety of gifts. Traditionally the dunti contains dresses, jewelry, coffee, and a lump of sugar, which symbolizes the sweetness of the honeymoon.

Most Albanian women marry in their teens. After marriage, a woman becomes a member of her husbands family and must obey her mate. Traditionally, women do not eat at the same table with men, and they do not express their opinions on political or social matters. This does not mean that Albanians do not respect women however. An old Albanian proverb states: "The hand that has hurt a woman is unfit for anything in the world."

Since the end of World War II, many women have entered the work force and are beginning to receive equal treatment in Albanian society. By 1972, women represented 40 percent of Albanian workers. The government provided day-care centers to care for the children of working mothers. Departing from tradition, Albanian women also became involved in national politics. In 1970, 72 of the 740 deputies of the Albanian People's Assembly were women.

The Albanian lifestyle is not elaborate. Historically, rural Albanians spent most of their time outdoors and took shelter only when the weather forced them to. As a result, the staples of their diet are simple foods that they can easily prepare in the open— cornbread, vegetables, and cheese. Although Albanians raise livestock, meat is a luxury reserved for festive occasions.

Because of Albania's proximity to Greece and the influence of the Turkish Empire, Albanian cuisine is virtually identical to

This woman is engaged in embroidery, a popular Albanian handicraft.

Turkish and Greek food. *Pilaf,* a rice dish that originated in Turkey, is a favorite in the Albanian diet. Albanian food is highly spiced and lavishly doused with olive oil. When meat is eaten, it is usually lamb, prepared "Albanian style," with garlic, onions, pepper, salt, and paprika.

Homemade wine, called *raki,* has a taste similar to dry Italian wine and is usually served with meals. Brandy and beer are also popular, although Albanians are not heavy drinkers. All the liquor drunk in Albania is made within the country's borders. Another favorite drink is Turkish coffee. This thick, black liquid, prepared over a stove or campfire, is served in small cups and is much stronger than the coffee drunk by Westerners. Its taste is similar to espresso, the strong Italian coffee.

In addition to cuisine, many other aspects of Albanian life

reflect a Turkish influence. Many Albanian men still wear baggy trousers with bright red or gold sashes around their waists. They also occasionally wear a white *fez*, a Turkish hat made of wool or felt. The traditional outfit for an Albanian woman is a wide, brightly-colored skirt that tapers to trousers at the ankles, a white muslin blouse, and a vest embroidered in gold thread. The style of an outfit customarily denoted its wearer's native region—and often his clan. Until the end of World War II, Albanian country women wore veils over their faces whenever they appeared in public.

Although Western-style clothing prevails today in the cities and towns, Albanians still frown on some Western fashions. Short skirts, blue jeans, tight-fitting trousers, and makeup are taboo. Young students dress much as their parents do. Girls wear dresses or skirts, and boys wear conservative trousers and plain shirts. Traditions die hard in Albania, and it is not uncommon for an

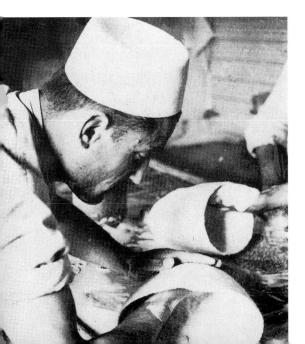

This man is shaping a fez, a wool or felt hat that forms a distinctive part of native male dress.

The Albanian treg, or marketplace, remains unchanged.

Albanian man to wear a Western-style suit and tie—and a fez on his head.

Although Albania has several large and bustling cities, most Albanians live in small towns or villages of fewer than 1,000 inhabitants. A typical town has narrow, winding streets and a large bazaar area called a *treg*. Peasants from the countryside come to the tregs to sell produce and other wares to the townspeople. The treg was one of the few aspects of Albanian life that remained unchanged after the Communist government took over. Albanian farmers could keep the money they earned selling their wares at the treg. As in most of Europe, the bazaar is a social center, and townspeople descend on the treg to meet their neighbors as well as to make purchases.

Because Albanians do not have a lot of excess income to spend

Oxcarts are still a common method of transportation in Albania.

on luxuries, entertainment is not a priority. The center of Albanian social life is the *konak*, or coffeehouse. Inside the konak, Albanians of all ages sit gossiping and drinking coffee. Another meeting place is the town square, where people gather at dusk to socialize. Each square has one or more *kiosks* (small newsstands) offering cigarettes, soft drinks, and local newspapers for sale.

Albania's large cities offer more varied entertainment. In Tirana, young people go to the park or stroll on the boulevards. Each night many people crowd into the National Library or go to the Palace of Culture to see an art exhibit. Tirana also has a few movie theaters, several playhouses, an opera house, and theaters that offer folklore programs. A typical date for a young city couple is a movie and a stroll through the park.

Only a few Albanians own their own automobile and there are only 58,000 passenger cars in the entire country. Many Albanians travel by bicycle. Such a great number of Albanians pedal their way around town that a policeman must direct bicycle traffic at dusk in Tirana's Scanderbeg Square. Public buses and taxicabs are also available, but few Albanians use them. Horses and donkeys are still common forms of transportation. Although there are rail lines to and from Tirana and other large cities, most Albanians have no use for them. In most cases, railroads transport goods.

Soccer is the most popular sport in Albania and it participates in international soccer competitions. Another popular sport is basketball. In Shkodër, a basketball game can draw more than 2,000 spectators into the Shkodër stadium, which was formerly an Orthodox cathedral.

7

The Economy

Approximately 50 percent of all Albanians make their living by farming or raising livestock. Although the use of modern farm machinery is increasing, many Albanians still use wooden plows, sickles, and waterwheels. Because agricultural exports are so vital to the Albanian economy, the government is encouraging the use of modern technology to produce better products in less time.

Sheep, goats, and cattle provide the main sources of income for Albania's mountain people; one-quarter of Albania's land is pastureland. It is not uncommon for herds of livestock to graze outside the capital city of Tirana. Albanians raise most of this livestock for export in the form of live animals and such animal products as leather goods, wool, and dairy products.

Albania's most fertile land lies along the coastal plain near the Adriatic Sea, but after 1945 the government tried to increase grain production by reclaiming the rocky, infertile land around the coast. In 35 years, Albania doubled its amount of cultivated land. The country's major crops are grains—farmers harvest 537,000

Much of Albania's industry continues to revolve around agriculture.

tons each year. They also cultivate potatoes, sugar beets, vegetables, and tobacco. Smokers have long favored Albanian tobacco because of its aroma and flavor. Some table fruit, wine grapes, vegetable oil, and olives are exported to other southeastern European countries. Albania trades with Italy, the Czech Republic, Turkey, Greece, Germany, and Bulgaria.

Forests cover more than 43 percent of Albania, and the country exports beech, fir, chestnut, oak, lime, and poplar wood. It also exports manufactured wood products, such as plywood and furniture. Unfortunately, Albania has harvested its most valuable tree, the walnut, out of existence.

After 1945, the government tried to increase its industrial output. One of its methods was to use machinery 24 hours a day. Manufacturing plant employees usually worked three shifts, and the average factory worker added overtime to his 48-hour, 6-day work week. In the 1970s some 40 percent of the population worked in industry or commerce. Since the economy collapsed in 1997 many of Albania's factories have closed and industrial and agricultural output have decreased.

Although Illyrians mined copper, asphalt, and silver in Albania as far back as the 4th century A.D., the country did not begin extensive mining until after World War II. Today, it exports the chrome, copper ore, pyrite, iron nickel ore, bauxite, gypsum, and limestone that abound in the northern and northeastern mountains.

Vast reserves of crude oil and natural gas lie beneath Albania's surface. The country exports much of its oil and refines the rest at

Albanian workers tap the country's vast reserves of crude oil.

a refinery near Elbasan. Its natural gas reserves are more plentiful than its crude oil, but it has not built enough pipelines to distribute the gas within the country.

Perhaps Albania's most powerful energy source is its many rivers. The great waterfalls in the mountain regions provide hydroelectric power. The plants at Ulze and Tirana generate most of the electricity for the nation. Today, power lines run up the steep mountains of northern Albania, bringing light to the ancient stone forts of the Ghegs. Albania generates so much power that it sells excess electricity to other Eastern European countries.

The Albanian currency is the *lek,* with 148 leks equal to one U.S. dollar. Albanians salaries are quite low by American standards. The cost of food is prohibitive and many items are scarce. Many of the major necessities are not available to Albanians. Their clothing is very expensive. A man's suit could cost a month's salary for a farmer or factory worker. The government regulates rents, so that no Albanian family pays more than 5 percent of his family's income for housing. Unfortunately, there is a shortage of housing, particularly in the cities. Many young married couples live with their parents because they cannot find homes of their own.

In most families, both husband and wife work. Although their houses are plain and poorly furnished by Western standards. Because of the hardships the country endured in over a half-century–World War II, two earthquakes, a drought, and the restrictions of a closed, Communist state–Albania is the poorest country in Europe.

8

Education

After the end of World War II, Albania made great strides in education. In 1938, it was estimated that more than 80 percent of the population was illiterate. At the turn of the century, the only schools in Albania were private, and most gave instruction only in the Turkish language. Only two Catholic schools taught in Albanian, in bold defiance of a Turkish law banning all use of the language. Until the 1920s, there was no public school system nor single college or university in Albania. Those who wanted an education had to go elsewhere in Europe or to the United States. After the war, the government introduced mandatory, free education programs. In 1980, Albania had an 80 percent literacy rate and by 1990 it was 92 percent.

The long years of Turkish rule greatly hampered Albanian education. Under King Zog I, the Albanian government sought to increase and expand education but the greatest educational success came under the Communist regime that took over in 1946. Between 1945 and 1965, the government increased the number of elementary schools from 928 to 2,481. Although in 1945 only some 54,000 Albanian children attended elementary school, by 1965 more than 227,500 were enrolled and the number of secondary school students rose from 2,500 to 50,794. Today Albania is trying to bring its education system up to European standards. Kindergartens are very popular and there are now 3,000 in Albania with 59 percent of all children now attending before going on to the primary schools. Some 70 percent of Albanian children now attend high school and a curriculum is being devised to help more of them go on to higher education.

School is compulsory between ages seven and 15. After completing four years of schooling, a child goes on for four or eight more years. One building houses all grades; the average school includes a kindergarten, primary classes, an evening school, an industrial and agricultural school, and a teacher training school.

Those who get into college usually go to the University of Tirana, Albania's only major university. Founded in 1957, the University of Tirana offers degrees in engineering, political science, geology, history, economics, medicine, and natural sciences. Five other cities have a small university and there is an Academy of Fine Arts in Tirana. Today over 25 percent of high school graduates are accepted at a university.

Once students are admitted they decide what they will study. Albania's "five-year plans" have determined how many doctors, engineers, geologists, scientists, and teachers it will require each year, and this helps to guide students into the course of study that best suits the country's needs. Students at the university spend long hours each day in classes.

Rugged mountains rising to a height of 6,000 feet (1,800 meters) dominate Albania's capital city of Tirana.

In educational matters, Albanians make no distinction between men and women. Immediately after World War II, the government encourage women to become literate and held free courses in reading and writing for more than 240,000 Albanian women. By 1970, 36 percent of students at the university in Tirana were women. Women receive not only equal opportunity but also equal responsibility. Women as well as men must take military training and serve in the armed forces. And when a group of Albanian students digs the foundation for a house or lays railroad track, women work side by side with men.

9

Arts and Culture

In a country so long oppressed, it is amazing that a distinctive Albanian culture has survived. The Turkish Empire made every effort to eradicate the unique Albanian flavor of the land it conquered. The repressive policies of the Turkish rulers forbade all written Albanian and permitted only Turkish or Greek to be used. For centuries the Albanian language survived only in the spoken form. A standardized alphabet did not come into use until the 20th century, and no Albanian dictionary was published until 1954.

The first literary ventures in the Albanian language came from a colony of Albanians who settled in Italy in the 15th century after the Turks had conquered their homeland. Consisting mainly of religious tracts, these early writings are important not for their literary merit but because they provided a basis for further development of the written language. The oldest document in Albanian is a short baptismal sentence believed to have been written in 1462 and preserved in Florence, Italy. In about 1555, what

Clinging to a mountainside in Berat, these buildings display typical examples of modern Albanian architecture and design.

is thought to be the first book printed in the Albanian language appeared. Printed in Venice, it is a compendium of church rituals. Today, this volume and other early Albanian religious texts are part of the Vatican Library.

In 1635 Francisus Blanchus compiled a Latin-Albanian lexicon containing about 5,000 words and considerable information about the Albanian language. This was the first Albanian word book. The first known Albanian grammar book appears to have been issued in Rome around 1715. But it was not until more than 100 years later, in 1827 that a Greek bishop of Albanian descent published an Albanian-language version of the New Testament.

The work of Konstandin Kristoforidhi (1827-1895), who came from Elbasan in the heart of Albania, constituted another major development in the language. After Kristoforidhi completed his education, the London Bible Society commissioned him to translate the Old and New Testaments into Albanian. While traveling through Albania, he collected words and phrases spoken in different parts of the region. From this material he compiled a Greek-Albanian dictionary, carefully correlating every word with the locality in which it was used. This important work was published in 1904, nine years after Kristoforidhi's death.

The Turks and the Greeks had always considered the Albanian language to be merely a crude, peasant dialect. The Turks had forbidden the printing of Albanian texts. An old Turkish proverb says that "the Albanian books had been eaten by the cow." But Kristoforidhi's Albanian bible showed world scholars that Albanian was more than an insignificant dialect. It proved beyond a doubt that the language was dynamic, rich in vocabulary, and capable of expressing intricate ideas. Today, scholars trace the Albanian language to the ancient Illyrian. Because of the country's many foreign occupations, Albanian also contains words and phrases from the Latin, Greek, Turkish, and Slavic languages.

Perhaps the most influential author in Albania's history was Naim Bey Frasheri (1846-1900), who was born in the little town of Frasheri, from which he took his name. Naim and his two equally brilliant brothers, Abdul and Sami, were descendants of an impoverished aristocratic family in southern Albania. Sami wrote an encyclopedia in Turkish and several volumes in

Albanian, chief among them a history of Albania, *Shqiperia Ch'ka Qene, Ch'eshte E Ch'do Të Jette* (Albania: past, present, and future). Sami Bey Frasheri was also the author of the first stage play to be written in the Albanian language. The drama had as its theme the bessa, or tribal word of honor.

The brothers were champions of the downtrodden Albanian people and threw themselves into the struggle for liberation from Turkey. Naim Bey Frasheri's voluminous works, written in the Albanian language, cover a variety of subjects. They include elementary school books, histories, poetry, and philosophical tracts. His greatest work is *Istori e Skenderbeut* (History of Scanderbeg). Written in verse, it is more than 12,000 stanzas long.

Naim Frasheri used simple, colloquial language, so that even the uneducated could understand his books. The Albanian peasants loved his works. Most peasants could not read, but the few who were literate cherished whatever books they could obtain,

Men celebrate fete days by wearing elaborate Scanderbeg jackets.

especially those by Naim Bey Frasheri. Since the Turks prohibited the Albanian language, the peasants hid volumes of Frasheri's work in secret places. Whenever possible, literate peasants would read aloud to neighbors and friends. The plots and simple ideas of these books passed into the stock of Albanian folklore. In this way, Albanian peasants maintained contact with their ethnic heritage.

Because of repression by the Turkish government and the Greek Orthodox Church, theater was slow to develop in Albania. After independence in 1912, however, it made its appearance. But subsequent years proved so politically tumultuous that its growth

Under King Zog, the Albanian people began to develop a national consciousness.

was halted. When the Communists came to power in 1945, they realized the potential of theater as an instrument of political and social indoctrination, and in 1949, they established a professional theater in Shkoder. Since then, numerous professional and amateur groups have sprung up throughout the country, performing dramas, comedies, variety shows, and puppet plays.

The Communist government made an effort to provide financial support for writers and artists. Although it allowed little contact with foreign performers, such as opera companies or musical and dance troupes, theaters were established in the cities. Tirana has an Albanian symphony orchestra, a national ballet, and a cultural center. Plays usually express a romantically patriotic theme.

Some old Albanian traditions have penetrated today's theater. For example, custom forbids women to appear on stage, so men play the feminine parts.

Today, Albanian Americans in America produce most Albanian-language theater. When Bishop Fan Noli came to the United States after Ahmet Zogu ousted him from Albania in 1924, he was most impressed by his countrymen's need to gain access to a wider range of drama. Noli began a long series of translations of classical writings into Albanian. He completed the first Albanian translation of the Greek Orthodox church service and later penned Albanian versions of several Shakespearean dramas, including *Othello, Hamlet, King Lear, Julius Caesar,* and *Macbeth.* He also translated several plays by Norwegian playwright Henrik Ibsen and selections from American writers Henry Wadsworth Longfellow and Edgar Allan Poe.

Albania has a rich tradition of folk music. Heroic and lyric songs, usually accompanied by folk instruments, have passed down from generation to generation. In the mountains of the north, the *lahute* (lute), a stringed instrument, is popular. Other Albanian folk instruments include the *roja*, a type of bagpipe, and the *tupan*, which is similar to the tambourine. Many towns have orchestras, called *saze*, usually consisting of four or five instruments, which provide music for folk dances, weddings, and other special occasions.

Albanian music finds its expression in the melodies accompanying the folk tales and legends of the people. Albanians call all poems songs *(kenge)*, and set every poem to music. These songs are usually variations on heroic and amorous themes and are often bawdy, although Albanians are usually quite conservative. Most Albanian songs are unknown outside the town or locality where they originated. Before the 1945 Communist takeover, however, a few Albanian songs were recorded. Today, those who study folklore consider these recordings great treasures.

Shortly after World War I, Thomas Nassi, a naturalized American of Albanian descent, returned to his native land and organized a band that eventually became the Royal Band of Albania under King Zog. Nassi traveled throughout the country listening to peasants sing their songs, and he transcribed dozens of them. He found that each folk song, regardless of the region from which it emanated, had a simple central theme that was repeated and developed as the song progressed. For example, each Albanian folk song is begun by a tenor. Then, when he has finished the first passage and is beginning the second, a baritone joins in, singing the first passage over again. The baritone continues to follow one phrase behind the tenor while the rest of the group supports the theme, increasing in volume and speed as it harmonizes with the ever-changing chords provided by the two singers.

Generally, Albanians of the old school look with disdain upon professional musicians. Only Gypsies, who make up about 2.5 percent of the population, play music for money. A typical Gypsy musical band consists of a clarinet, a flute, and a small portable organ with two keys plugged down, emitting a droning bass sound.

Kristro Kono is perhaps the only significant composer of post-World War II Albania. In the 1950s and 1960s, Kono wrote several songs, some of which he dedicated to Stalin. His most noted orchestral pieces are *Fantazi Shqipatre* (Albanian fantasies) and *Agimi* (Dawn).

Albania established its first art school in Tirana in the 1930s, but the curriculum did not go beyond the fundamentals. Consequently, talented students had to go abroad to expand their education. Under the Communist government, the state supported artists and sculptors. But this support did not come without a price. Albanian artists had to confine their work to themes approved by the government: workers, peasants, partisan heroes, youth working on agricultural and industrial projects, soldiers, and liberated women going about various activities.

Cinematography is another area that did not develop until after World War II. During the Italian occupation, from 1939 to 1945, a joint Italian-Albanian film company produced documentary films in Tirana. When Albania became Communist, the Soviet Union initially assisted in providing film equipment and training, but when Albania and the Soviet Union terminated relations in 1961, the Soviets left Albania and took their film equipment with them.

The Albanians tried to produce films without foreign help. The government made an effort to increase film production and to expand facilities for showing movies to the public. Each year, a few full-length films and a greater number of documentaries appear. The government often makes literary works into art films. It also imports films from other countries and dubs them into Albanian.

10

Albania Today

Today, Albania is a struggling nation. Because of their history of conquests and repression, many Albanians feel that most outsiders cannot be trusted. Only recently has the government opened its borders to the outside world. Prior to that Albania

This war memorial in downtown Scutari honors Albanian soldiers killed in action during World War II.

refused any assistance or economic investments from foreign sources. Even when an earthquake hit northern Albania in 1979, the country refused offers of aid from other countries and from relief agencies such as the International Red Cross. A banner in Scanderbeg Square in Tirana read: "Without any foreign aid and any credit from abroad, we rely entirely on our own forces." But this isolationist policy delayed the country's economic and cultural growth. Albania finally realized that without outside aid and ideas it would stagnate and its people would continue to live in poverty.

Albanians may now travel beyond the Albanian border. The Western world's knowledge about Albania is increasing and since its borders opened in the early 1990s economic aid and investment have come into the country. But Albania remains Europe's poorest nation and it will take more than a few years to recover from the isolation of decades. Under Communism the state owned every business in Albania, controlled all konaks, kiosks, taxicabs, hotels, and restaurants, as well as all newspapers and magazines. Because of this it will take a while to reap the benefits of privitization of businesses and a free-market economy.

Because every word in the pages of magazines and newspapers had to be approved by government agencies and no magazines or newspapers from any other part of the world entered the country for more than 40 years, Albania did not have the benefits of sharing ideas with the outside world. But communication is increasing. Although Albanians cannot afford many luxuries, some now own television sets and many have radios on which they can hear daily broadcasts. There are now about 400 independent newspapers and magazines being published and foreign publications are sold alongside them. Telephone service is still obsolete and many of the wires have fallen or been cut to make fences in the villages.

After World War II, the government's extensive health care program dramatically increased Albanian life expectancy. In 1940, the average Albanian lived only to 38, but by 1980 life expectancy had jumped to 68 years where it has remained. Modern health care has even reached the isolated mountain regions. In 1994, there was one doctor for every 552 people, not far behind the ratio of much more developed countries. And Albania has more hospital beds per capita—one for every 133 persons—than many other countries.

Albania has an army, a navy, and air force. All young Albanians—both men and women—must serve two years in a

An Albanian farmer feeds her livestock. Most Albanian farms are small.

Albanian president Rexhap Mejdani paid repeated visits to the Kosovo refugee camps and encouraged his people to open their homes to them.

branch of the military. During the Communist years, the government trained almost every citizen, so that in the event of an attack the entire nation could mobilize instantly. Schools, factories, farms, and even offices regularly conducted military exercises. Throughout the country, in the mountains, the fields, and the city

92

parks, steel-and-concrete bunkers were set up in case of foreign invasion.

Since the fall of Communism and Albania's opening of its borders it has begun to participate in the world community. It has improved economic and cultural ties, and received outside aid

Ethnic Albanian refugees from Kosovo cross the border into Albania seeking refuge from the Serbian army.

and support. Albania is no longer isolated from the rest of the world.

The economic crises of the late 1990s set Albania's progress back. But it is beginning to recover from that and the recent crisis in Kosovo has brought Albania to the international headlines and hopefully it will now receive more international aid.

Albania's hopes for the future must now rely on the endurance and determination of its citizens both in the country and outside of it to take their place as a vital part of the international community. The rugged mountain people have endured much during their long and turbulent history, and their trials have imbued them with conviction and strength and the courage to endure.

GLOSSARY

arnaut	Specialized soldiers in the Turkish army
barjaks	Clans comprised of many family units (*fis*) who live and work as a group
baryaktar	Leader of a barjak or clan
bessa	Strictly held to word of honor given in Albanian clans
beys	Local rulers under the Turkish sultans
Canon of Lek	Ancient code of laws of the Albanian clans
cifliks	Hereditary estates ruled by Muslim overlords during the Turkish Empire's rule in Albania
dunti	Bridal hope chest filled with a variety of gifts by the groom's family
fis	Family unit within a clan
gyak	Blood feud; code by which male Albanians were honor bound to avenge the killing of a relative by killing his murderer or someone in his clan
Illyria	The ancient name of the area now called Albania
konak	Coffeehouse; the center of the social life of an Albanian town

nationalism	The desire for an independent, unified country and loyalty to that country
pilaf	A baked rice dish common to Albania, Greece, and Turkey
pleqet	Tribal supreme court of the historic clans in Albania
raki	Homemade Albanian wine
treg	Marketplace

INDEX

97

98

DATE			